My 21-Day

RITE-OF-PASSAGE

Journal

Sherry Lee Heeb

WESTBOW·
PRESS
A DIVISION OF THOMAS NELSON
& ZONDERVAN

WestBow Press books may be ordered through booksellers or by contacting:

WestBow Press
A Division of Thomas Nelson & Zondervan
1663 Liberty Drive
Bloomington, IN 47403
www.westbowpress.com
1 (866) 928-1240

ISBN: 978-1-4908-0986-1 (sc)
ISBN: 978-1-4908-0987-8 (e)

Library of Congress Control Number: 2013918913

Printed in the United States of America.

WestBow Press rev. date: 2/3/2014

My 21-Day

RITE-OF-PASSAGE

Journal

Lovingly dedicated to my daughter Natasha Joi,
whose gorgeous smile melts snow and hearts.
She changes the world every moment she's in it
in a 4good4ever way
and makes my heart dance.
Joi, Joi, whatever the passage, we are in this together forever.
Go get 'em, girl!

What are the 4good4ever journals?

They are a series of twenty-one-day journals, each with a different theme but the same goal: to keep our awareness on love, life, and light that will allow us to bring more joy and meaning into our lives.

How do I begin the journals?

You can choose any one journal theme, do them all, or do the same one repeatedly. Begin any day you like, skip a day, or go straight through.

Make up your own rules.

Why are the journals recommended to be done with someone else?

The journals are suggested to be done with a journal friend because having someone you can talk with during the process is important and more fun.

Why do the journals suggest using a ribbon as a symbol of my commitment?

The ribbons are a reminder that you're making a twenty-one-day commitment 4good4ever. Tie them on your wrist (with your journal friend), on your purse, on your bed lamp, or wherever you like.

What do I do during the twenty-one-day journal?

Each day has a focus word, quotes, and questions. You can write in your journal and cut out the quotes—or not!

Each day, you do three things 4good4ever. You choose the things you do, from starting a new job, sending a thank-you card, or giving yourself a time-alone break.

All acts, large and small, are valuable.

What's the purpose of three 4good4ever acts a day?

One 4good4ever act is dedicated to love, one to life, and one to light. The habit of inviting love, life, and light into our lives in a daily ritual brings powerful and positive change.

Do I do 4good4ever things for myself or for others?

Doing good only for others or doing good only for yourself never works, so just do what feels good, and the balance will come. If you're going through a difficult time, it may be useful to do more good for yourself. As you start feeling better, you'll naturally feel like giving more to others.

What does "4good4ever 'Round the World" mean?

We're joining acts 4good4ever to symbolically circle the world.

What are the facts of circling the world?

The world is 25,000 miles around at the equator, and there are 5,280 feet in a mile, so it takes 132 million feet to circle the world. With each person stretching out his or her arms six feet, three feet to either side as if holding hands, we need 22 million acts of 4good4ever to circle the globe.

How many 4good4ever acts will it take to circle the world?

Each person doing three 4good4ever acts in one journal for twenty-one days equals 63 acts. The journals are done in pairs, so this equals 126 acts 4good4ever per journal pair. We need 174,603 pairs of people doing the twenty-one-day journals to circle the world in acts 4good4ever. Join the circle.

Rite of Passage

This is the first of the 4good4ever journals. Thru all the changes ahead in our lives, one constant we take with us is ourselves. What we get out of life is what we focus on. This journal strengthens who we are, what we want, and where we are going.

In every life there will be:

Wild Cards—unexpected things happen.
Speed Bumps—so slow down and keep going.
Land Mines—but you can run for cover and be flexible.
Snafus—which will teach you to be steady and get stronger.
Tsunamis—which will teach you to recover from loss.
Fences—but you can hurdle these.
Walls—and these will teach you to climb.

4good4ever is:

ACTIONS, PROMISES, LISTENING,
WORDS SPOKEN, TALKING, PHONE CALLS,
VOLUNTEERING, WORDS WRITTEN,
LETTERS, CARDS, GIFTS, BLESSINGS!

Love—Life—Light

Everything we do matters: sending, giving, receiving, inviting,
sharing, driving, helping, baking, hoping, smiling, hugging,
surprising, asking, praying, watching, laughing, planting,
encouraging, picking up, holding, believing, making,
keeping playing, dancing, sharing, reading, writing,
talking, letting go, listening, and celebrating!

LOVE
There are no great things, only small things with great love.   —Mother Teresa

LIFE
I long to accomplish a great and noble task, but it is my chief duty to accomplish small tasks as if they were great and noble.
                                                        —Helen Keller

LIGHT
Despite everything, I believe that people are really good at heart.   —Anne Frank

To everything there is a season and a time to every purpose
under heaven: A time to be born, a time to let go; A time to
plant, a time to harvest; A time to weep, a time to laugh;
A time to heal, a time to dance; A time to keep, a time
to cast away; A time to love and a time of peace.—Ecclesiastes 3:1-8

Treat yourself with the same dignity and respect you give others.
Lucky Numbers 34, 27, 11, 6, 38, 40

This is my time under heaven and heaven on earth.

Dear Rite of Passage friends,

My daughter and I were finishing our Chinese lunches when our fortunes arrived. We read them aloud. Mine read, "Treat yourself with the same dignity and respect you give others."

"You should actually do that," my daughter said.

"What do you mean?"

"You're so nice to other people, so why not to yourself?"

I decided to do that immediately. That night, I started a list and decided to give myself permission to be completely happy. The first five on the list were easy; the next seven very exciting and freeing; by seventeen I was giddy. Soon there were twenty-one!

I called it my rite of passage. I had lived long enough with those walls of limitations. I felt that the next half of my life deserved a new path. I put closure on a relationship that had been poisoning my life for years. I stopped allowing people and conditions to deplete me and cause doubt in my decisions. I began a deeper daily walk in my faith.

The worse the passage, the more welcome the port.—Thomas Fuller

Each day, you will receive ideas, so do what you want.

Today, do three things 4good4ever:

 for love, something from your heart

 for life, something that supports life

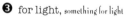 for light, something for light

My Rite of Passage

Week One

Day 1: Ask a *friend* to do the twenty-one-day journal with you, tie reminder ribbons, and write something you want in your life in twenty-one days.

Day 2: *Truth*—carry a rock

Day 3: *Light*—light a candle

Day 4: *Signs*—look for signs

Day 5: *I'm sorry*—wear a Band-Aid

Day 6: *Lucky*—find a penny/charm

Day 7: *Respect yourself*

DAY 1

MY RITE OF PASSAGE

Today, do three things 4good4ever for a friend.

❶ for love, something from your heart; hug a friend, send a friend a friendly text.

> Write it here:

❷ for life, something that supports life; invite a friend to coffee or lunch.

> Write it here:

❸ for light, something for light; tell a friend what she or he means to you.

> Write it here:

In the next twenty-one days, I want to:

- ○ be happier
- ○ be a closer friend
- ○ make new girlfriends/boyfriends
- ○ be a better daughter/son/relative
- ○ be a better parent
- ○ be a better roommate
- ○ be a better student
- ○ be healthier
- ○ _____

- ○ become committed, engaged, married
- ○ be a better wife/husband/boyfriend/girlfriend
- ○ change, close, or end a relationship
- ○ be a more concerned neighbor
- ○ be a more active citizen
- ○ be a better coworker, business owner
- ○ advance my career/creativity/education
- ○ exercise more
- ○ _____

—Cut————————Signs under Heaven————————————

Day 1:   We are each of us angels with only one wing. And we can only fly embracing each other.
                                                                          —Luciano DeCrescenzo

Friend

Winter, spring, summer, or fall,

all you have to do is call,

and I'll be there.

You've got a friend.

—Carole King

My best girlfriend died in February. It was snowing the day she died. She made a snow angel. I guess God called her home.
> —Deb, age twenty-seven; mother of two boys, loves tennis and babies

I met Kelly the first day at college standing in line for our ID cards. When my parents left, I was completely alone three thousand miles from home. I was so happy to have someone to eat lunch with! —Anna; freshman in college

I have felt alone all my life. I was married; now I'm divorced. I felt alone even when I was married. I want to change that.
> —Marie, age thirty-two; a career in finance, enjoys reading and biking

This is my time under heaven. The choices I make, the chances I take, determine my destiny.

In the next twenty-one days, I want to: _____

_____

My Personal Fortune!

DAY 2

ONLY THE TRUTH IS REAL

First, start with me!

In the next twenty-one days, I want to:

- ☐ Find something real and good about myself
- ☐ Stop lies now
- ☐ Live in truth

I can be really myself (at least for the next twenty-one days).

My relationship with myself is how I begin every new relationship.

With your journal friend, discuss if your emotions portray the truth about you.
I am usually:

○ happy	○ fearful	○ forgiving	○ jealous
○ sad	○ resentful	○ kind	○ optimistic
○ hopeful	○ angry	○ helpful	○ cautious
○ _____	○ _____	○ _____	○ _____

DO: Find a stone and carry it in your pocket.

A stone is strong, and the truth makes you stronger.

The truth may hurt, but lies can kill you. —*Mort Sahl*

—Cut————————Signs under Heaven————————————
Day 2:   The day we see the truth and cease to speak is the day we begin to die.
                                                              —Martin Luther King Jr.

Truth

> In matters of style, swim with the current;
>
> In matters of principle, stand like a rock.
>
> —Thomas Jefferson

My boyfriend of three years lied to me about everything. Even when I knew he was lying, I wanted to believe he was sorry so I could believe he still loved me. Then I realized if he really loved me, he wouldn't lie. I didn't want to be in love with a liar anymore, so I cut the line.
                                        —Rachael, age twenty-three; college graduate looking for a job

Kelly and I pledged the same sorority, and we both got in! We're now roommates. I miss my family, but now I have someone I can trust and talk to.   —Anna, sorority sister; loves movies

Our lives improve only when we take chances, and the first and most difficult risk we can take is to be honest with ourselves.   — Walter Anderson

Do: Three things 4good4ever (4 Truth):

❶ **for love,** something from your heart; tell yourself the truth, listen to a friend.

> Write it here: _____

❷ **for life,** something that supports life; ask a friend to listen to you.

> Write it here: _____

❸ **for light,** make a list of truthful people you trust. Are you on the list?

> Write it here: _____

DAY 3

THIS LITTLE LIGHT OF MINE

First, shine my light!

The saddest day hath gleams of light.

—Sarah Winnemuca

What do I focus on? What do I have or don't have?

- ○ I accept not being perfect.
- ○ I work on changing what I can.
- ○ I accept my family.
- ○ _____

- ○ I accept being me.
- ○ I lighten up on myself.
- ○ I accept my past.
- ○ _____

The purpose of light is to enable us to see, to get rid of darkness. Light protects us from darkness and allows us to see what we are looking for.

DO: Light a candle and promise to see light in everything and everyone; it's only twenty-one days, for goodness' sake!

In the next twenty-one days, I want to:

Do your best and forget the rest.—*Tony Horton*

—Cut————————Signs under Heaven————————————

Day 3: It is at night that faith in light is most admirable. —Edmond Rostand

Light

> There are two ways of spreading light:
> to be the candle or the mirror reflecting it.
>
> —Edith Wharton

I wasted most of my whole life waiting for things to be perfect. They never were, and now I am in my eighties, and I just want to be happy. Most of the things I wanted never really mattered anyway. I've learned to love so many things over time. I love hot tea, funny movies, new slippers, and rainstorms.
— Nora, age eighty-three; just completed a knitathon for charity

I told Kelly things that happened between my ex-boyfriend and me. They were private, and I asked her not to tell anyone else. She told people and also said mean things about me. I'm so hurt, angry, and embarrassed. Why would she want to hurt me, especially when I thought we trusted each other? —Anna, sorority sister; loves dogs

I always wear yellow on dark days. That way I carry the sunshine with me!
—Jilly, age thirty-three; works in a spa, wants to visit a tropical island

Today, do three things 4good4ever (4 Light):

❶ for love, something from your heart; smile, look people in the eye, keep smiling.

   Write it here: _____

❷ for life, something that supports life; see light in the shadows, turn on a night light.

   Write it here: _____

❸ for light, something for light; light a candle, encourage someone and yourself.

   Write it here: _____

DAY 4

SIGNS FOR ME

First, look for signs, ask for signs.

Signs are everywhere, so see humor and love in signs.

You have to be willing to get happy about nothing.
    —*Andy Warhol*

What makes you happy?

- ○ naps
- ○ socializing
- ○ shopping
- ○ _____

- ○ sunsets
- ○ cooking
- ○ working out
- ○ _____

- ○ art
- ○ bubble baths
- ○ music
- ○ _____

- ○ holding hands
- ○ flowers/trees
- ○ reading/writing
- ○ _____

DO: Go out today asking and looking for signs. Ask your journal friend. You'll be amazed at what you find and what finds you.

In the next twenty-one days, I want to:

—Cut————————Signs under Heaven————————————

Day 4: What lies behind us and what lies ahead of us are tiny matters compared to what lies within us.
    —Henry David Thoreau

16

Signs

This is a true and very amazing story. If it hadn't happened to me, I wouldn't believe it. I was in the car with my boyfriend, and he was yelling at me, again. I don't even remember (honestly) what it was about. I was thinking, _I'm going to start crying._ I had to make a decision if I should leave him or not. I looked up at a sign in a gas station that read, "If anyone is looking for a sign from God, this is it." I packed all of my things in the morning and I have never talked to him since.

—S. L., age twenty-four; volunteer in women's shelters

I was afraid to talk to Kelly, but I knew I just had to. I told her I heard she had talked about me and said not only private things but also mean things about me. I asked her to apologize if she wanted to be friends again or roommates next year. She denies that she said anything, but that is just a lie.

—Anna, age twenty; college student, loves traveling

I was looking for some clarity on my career when I overheard a woman talking to her friend say, "I'm a lawyer; that's what I do, but that's not why I'm here."

—B.J.M., age sixty-one; actor in New York

Today, do three things 4good4ever (4 Signs):

❶ for love, something from your heart; look around your room for signs and what they mean to you.

　　　Write it here: _____

❷ for life, something that supports life; make a wish in a fountain and another for a friend.

　　　Write it here: _____

❸ for light, something for light; give a friend a lucky penny or charm.

　　　Write it here: _____

Happiness is the only good. The time to be happy is now.

The place to be happy is here.—Robert Ingersoll

17

DAY 5

"I'M SORRY"

Sorry starts with me.

To whom do I want to apologize?

    Do I feel someone owes me an apology?

        Stop hurting others and yourself and be brave. Ask for an apology you want.

            If you don't get it, move on; at least you asked.

Ways to say "I'm sorry":

- ○ write and mail a letter
- ○ write and don't mail a letter
- ○ call on the phone or text
- ○ say or write a prayer
- ○ _____

- ○ talk to the person face-to-face
- ○ send a greeting card
- ○ talk to a trusted friend
- ○ write a note and/or e-mail
- ○ _____

I choose to be happy over perfect. I choose to be _____

With your journal friend, remind each other to heal resentment, sadness, and bitterness. Promise to say and receive "I'm sorry" for the next twenty-one days even over the little things—maybe especially over the little things.

In the next twenty-one days, I want to:

—Cut———————————Signs under Heaven———————————

Day 5:   So let us not talk falsely now, the hour is getting late.   —Bob Dylan

"I'm Sorry"

It is easier to leave angry words unspoken

than to mend a heart those words have broken.

My mom makes me say "I'm sorry" to my brother all the time. She says it's good practice because in life, everyone makes mistakes and you need to own up to them. Sometimes she apologizes to me, and it makes me feel good that she cares enough about me to say "I'm sorry" and just to know she cares about my feelings.

—Darla, age fifteen; loves soccer, spaghetti, and boys (in that order)

It was so sad that Kelly never admitted what she said or said she was sorry. She lives on a different floor now, but I still hear all the drama. I guess the latest is that she invited someone else's beau to the formal. I'm glad she can't hurt me in the same way because I know what she is all about now. I have a new roommate, and we seem more compatible.

—Anna, age twenty-one; junior in college, medical major

I told my husband before we got married that he would have to be able and willing to say he was sorry to me. I didn't want to be married to a man who couldn't say "I'm sorry." He's become quite good at it! No kidding! LOL.

—Lillian, age thirty; veterinarian, married four years, lives on a farm

Today, do three things 4good4ever (4 I'm Sorry):

1 for love, something from your heart; ask, "Can I say I'm sorry about something?"

Write it here:_____

2 for life, something that supports life; say, "I'm sorry that I hurt you," to someone or yourself.

Write it here:_____

3 for light, something for light; write an "I'm sorry" card to someone or yourself.

Write it here:_____

DAY 6

"I'm Lucky!"

Only those who dare to fail greatly can never achieve greatly
—Robert Kennedy

All things are difficult before they are easy.

—Thomas Fuller

What's Important to me?

- ○ honesty
- ○ family
- ○ giving back
- ○ _____

- ○ health
- ○ friends
- ○ respect
- ○ _____

- ○ freedom
- ○ forgiveness
- ○ love
- ○ _____

- ○ laughter
- ○ education
- ○ compassion
- ○ _____

DO: Find a lucky penny/four-leaf clover or charm and carry it with you.

With your journal friend, share stories and review your Personal Fortune from Day 1 in your Journal.

In the next twenty-one days, I want to:

—Cut————————Signs under Heaven————————————————

Day 6: Luck is when preparation meets opportunity.   —Seneca

"I'm Lucky"

Miracles happen to those who believe in them.

—Bernard Berenson

My daughter and I were shopping in a women's clothing store. I was looking at a jacket when the saleswoman said it was on a special discount. While I purchased the jacket, she said there was a special promotion; for that price point, I could choose a free accessory. As we walked out, my daughter asked, "Why are you so lucky?" Right then, we looked down and there was a two-dollar bill on the floor in front of us!

—S. L., age fifty-two; works on children's self-esteem projects

College life is so stressful. Classes, professors' whims, girl drama, boy drama, and just living drama. I guess the average college student sends five hundred text messages a day. Who's average anyway? I don't know how we do it some days. In twelve days (but who's counting?), I go home for Thanksgiving break. A sorority sister who can't get home is coming home with me. I feel lucky.   —Anna, age twenty-two; college senior, loves turkey with catsup

One day I found a penny, a nickel, and a quarter. Now that's pretty lucky!
—Natasha Goodman, age twenty; loves decorating, palm trees, and convertibles

Today, do three things 4good4ever (4 Luck):

❶ for love, something from your heart; imagine your very best and luckiest day.

Write it here: _____

❷ for life, something that supports life; expect lucky and good things to happen.

Write it here: _____

❸ for light, something for light; be thankful for all the lucky moments in your life.

Write it here: _____

DAY 7

First, Respect Yourself!

Get to know yourself. People and things in your life will come and go, but one thing you'll always have is you. Respect yourself, value yourself, and love yourself, all without judgment—it's only twenty-one days!

With your journal friend, share what you respect about each other.

In the next twenty-one days, I want to:

- ◯ enjoy my own company
- ◯ require others to respect me
- ◯ treat myself with respect
- ◯ say no when I want to
- ◯ do what is nurturing for me
- ◯ _____

- ◯ stand up for myself
- ◯ speak out to support myself
- ◯ list things I respect about me
- ◯ do the things I respect
- ◯ give away something that is no longer me
- ◯ _____

Today, do three things that respect yourself.

You've got to be original, because if you're like everyone else, what do they need you for?—Bernadette Peters

—Cut————————Signs under Heaven————————————————

Day 7:   Joy is not in things, it is in us.   —Richard Wagner

Respect Yourself

Learn to say no. It will be of more use to you than to be able to read Latin.

—Charles Haddon Spurgeon

My heart and what I send out (Fill it in to make it yours):

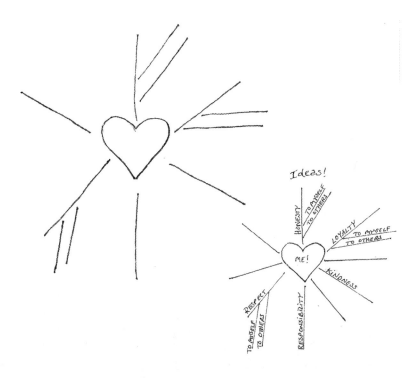

What is happiness except the simple harmony
between man and the life he leads?

—Albert Camus

23

Each day, there will be ideas, so do what you want.

Today, do three things 4good4ever:

❶ for love, something from your heart

❷ for life, something that supports life

❸ for light, something for light

My Rite of Passage

Week Two

DAY 8

MY RITE OF PASSAGE

*Until you make peace with who you are, you'll never
be content with what you have.—Doris Mortman*

Say "Thank you" all day, everywhere, for every reason.

Make a Gratitude List and write a thank-you note.

DO: Be thankful every minute; it's really fun and easy.

With your journal friend: share from your gratitude list.

In the next twenty-one days, I will be thankful for:

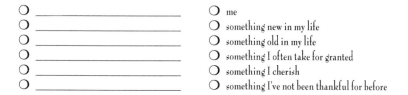

○ _____   ○ me
○ _____   ○ something new in my life
○ _____   ○ something old in my life
○ _____   ○ something I often take for granted
○ _____   ○ something I cherish
○ _____   ○ something I've not been thankful for before

—Cut———————————Signs under Heaven————————————

Day 8:   If you want to feel rich, just count all the things you have that money cannot buy.

—Anonymous

Gratitude

I think being grateful is a habit. I keep a little notebook on my bedside table. At night, or in the morning if I'm too tired, I write down something I'm thankful for. I've been doing this for thirty years now. It's real swell to look back.
—Evelyn, age seventy-six; grandmother of three, loves parades.

When I first met Kevin, I liked everything about him. He seemed so confident. He's tall—so am I—and he has brown eyes and kind of spiky hair. He was so interested in everything about me. He kept his arm around me the whole night when we were together. I was thinking, He could be the one!

—Emma, hairstylist; drives a moped to work

My mom makes me make a list of things I'm thankful for at Thanksgiving. She helps me remember things if I forget, but I always put Max, my dog, in big letters.
—Samantha, age eight, loves butterflies, math, and Max

Today, do three things 4good4ever (4 Gratitude):

❶ for love, something from your heart; keep adding to your thankful list; read it all day.

Write it here:_____

❷ for life, something that supports life; donate food, mittens, or shoes.

Write it here:_____

❸ for light, something for light; bless your family and friends, each and every one.

Write it here:_____

You have no cause for anything but gratitude and joy.

—Gautama Buddha

DAY 9

When Tears Come

First: Tears

❑ What hurts me?
❑ Why does this hurt so much?
❑ Remember, this too shall pass

DO: 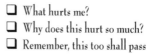 Let yourself cry; it can cleanse your heart and soul. Buy your favorite color Kleenex to remember the rainbow is coming.

With your journal friend, share what makes you cry.

In the next twenty-one days, I want to:

○ stop allowing others to hurt me   ○ listen to my heart
○ start believing in myself   ○ find ways to nurture myself
○ ask for help   ○ make changes for good
○ _____   ○ _____

Life begins on the other side of despair.
—Jean-Paul Sartre

—Cut————————Signs under Heaven————————————

Day 9:   The soul would have no rainbow if the eye had no tear.   —Anonymous

28

Tears

I had this boyfriend who always made me cry. One of my girlfriends would say, "You're so wasting your tears. Save your tears for something important." She was right. He was cruel, and now I see things that matter so much more.

—Jolie, age twenty-three; loves fishing and family reunions

Kevin and I have been inseparable for months now. Lately, he doesn't like me to go anywhere without him. I'm taking a computer class, and he makes fun of me. Sometimes he calls me hideous names. Yesterday, he pulled my hair and shoved me. He said he was just kidding around, but it didn't feel like it. I started crying hard. He hurt me inside and out.

—Emma; works in a hair salon, loves drawing

My brother is in the army, and last week, he was sent overseas to a war zone. When he left, I was sobbing and clinging to him. He pried my arms off his shoulders. If he dies, so will I.

— Marcia, age twenty; loves crossword puzzles and history

Today, do three things 4good4ever (4 Tears):

❶ **for love,** something from your heart; tell someone you trust what is hurting you.

   Write it here: _____

❷ **for life,** something that supports life; bring a friend some soup.

   Write it here: _____

❸ **for light,** something for light; ask someone how you can help him or her.

   Write it here: _____

DAY 10

First, Let Go!

I will give no more time of my life to someone or something I now let go; I will no longer let this hurt me, as I'm out of prison.

DO: Find a leaf. Leaves let go, and so can you.

>   With your journal friend, share something you let go.

If you love something, let it go.

If it comes back to you, it's yours. If it doesn't, it never was.

Don't try to control the uncontrollable. If you've tried your best to change something and continually met resistance, give up, at least for a while. Begin slowly to make the changes you want to make in yourself, but begin now.

In the next twenty-one days, I want to:

○ stop putting energy into what isn't working
○ leave the past in the past
○ choose what to think about and how to feel about it
○ _____
○ _____

—Cut————————————Signs under Heaven————————————Cut—
Day 10: When I let go of what I am, I become what I might be.   —Lao Tzu

Let Go

I thought it would be impossible to quit hating my ex, but I just decided no more poison, and that was it. If other people bring him up, I just say "Not interested," and it's over. Wow! I feel so free. I never thought I could feel this happy. —Tami, age thirty-nine; baker

Kevin says it's all my fault that we fight. At first, I didn't believe him, but now I'm not sure. He says I make him mad and do things on purpose to hurt him. I don't think that's true, but I'm so confused. I spend all my time trying not to make him mad or crying because I hate it when he yells at me.

—Emma, age twenty-four; loves mocha lattes

Today, do three things 4good4ever (4 Letting Go):

❶ for love, something from your heart; think of three things that stop you from being happy.

Write them here: _____

❷ for life, something that supports life; go somewhere new—dancing, a movie, a museum.

Write it here: _____

❸ for light, something for light; carry a photo or take one on your phone that makes you smile and show it to everyone.

Write it here: _____

How desperately we wish to maintain our trust in those we love. In the face of everything, we try to find reasons to trust. Because losing faith is worse than falling out of love.

—Sonia Johnson

DAY 11

First, Forgive!

Forgiving takes practice, so practice it. Forgiveness feels good, so do it. Forgiving is really for yourself.

DO: Forgiveness is a private thing— only you know if you're actually doing it.

Lies breed fear and anger; fear and anger breed distrust and hatred; distrust and hatred breed broken hearts, relationships, and families.

Truth, on the other hand, builds confidence and loyalty; confidence and loyalty build trust and love; trust and love build strong hearts, relationships, and families.

In the next twenty-one days, I want to ask myself:

○ Am I being honest and building trust and love? Truth strengthens relationships.
○ Am I lying and breeding distrust and hatred? Lies weaken relationships.
○ Are my relationships strong and healthy or broken and destructive?

—Cut————————Signs under Heaven————————————

Day 11: If a relationship is to evolve, it must go through a series of endings.   —Lisa Moriyama

Forgive

My marriage was a tsunami, and my divorce a tornado. Now I live in peaceful paradise. I should be a weather lady. Lol! In three years, my life went from a nightmare to a dream come true.
—Mary, age forty-three; freelance writer, loves concerts and the beach

Kevin says if I were a better girlfriend, everything would be perfect. I feel exhausted. I know that he loves me and that I should be happy such a great guy wants to be with me. I try so hard, and things seem okay for a while, but then he's mad again, and the whole cycle of calling me names and me crying starts all over again.   —Emma, aunt, to Addie, age two months

Today, do three things 4good4ever (4 Forgiving):

❶ **for love,** something from your heart; make a forgiveness ritual, take a day and forgive everyone including yourself.

    Write it here: _____

❷ **for life,** something that supports life; bake "forgiveness" cookies and share them.

    Write it here: _____

❸ **for light,** something for light; ask someone if you can "start over" together.

    Write it here: _____

Rest in the assurance of Truth's certain triumph.
—Edward Kimball

DAY 12

MY RITE OF PASSAGE

Reverse the Engines!

Live the life you've dreamed.—Henry David Thoreau

Knowing others is wisdom; knowing yourself is enlightenment.
—Lao Tzu

People in the Misery Box blame, shame, and hurt others because they can't feel pain or they want others to be as miserable as they are.

In the next twenty-one days, I want to:

List people in the misery box and leave them there.

○ _____

○ _____

○ _____

DO: Stop the misery box. Share your list. No blaming, shaming, or making everything someone else's fault; also, no receiving shame or blame.

—Cut—————————Signs under Heaven—————————————

Day 12: Those who are unhappy have no need for anything in this world but people capable of giving them attention. .   —Simone Weil

Reverse the Engines

Let nothing perturb you, nothing frighten you. All things pass. God does not change. Patience achieves everything.—Mother Teresa

I was so afraid to leave my job. I hated getting up in the morning, but I had too many bills to just quit. I started sending resumes and talking to people on nights and weekends. After ten months, it finally happened—I start my new job tomorrow. I'm an assistant in an art studio. Yippee!
— Carlen, age thirty-two; loves vintage clothes, local art, and collecting books

I can't keep doing this. I don't care what Kevin says anymore. Someone else can put up with his cruelty and name-calling. He blamed and shamed me for everything. Maybe he thinks he's better than me, but at least I'm smart enough to get rid of him. I think I'll need to get a new phone because he's harassing me. —Emma, age twenty-five; takes painting classes

Today, do three things 4good4ever (2 Reverse Engines):

❶ for love, something from your heart; give yourself a chance to be happy, and choose some good people to be around you.

Write it here:_____

❷ for life, something that supports life; take a workout/yoga/dance class.

Write it here:_____

❸ for light, something for light; wear your favorite color or dance.

Write it here:_____

DAY 13

My Wish

Wish for something *little* that could easily happen. Wish for something *bigger* just for the fun of it. Wish for something *huge* because it just might happen.

DO: Make a wishboard/collage that holds pictures of all the things you want to be and do.

> It's not what happens to you, but how you react to it that matters.—Epictetus

In the next twenty-one days, I want to:

○ be aware of how important every thought I have is and how every word I say affects my life
○ realize how my thoughts and words are ignited by my feelings
○ understand everything I give comes back to me
○ discipline myself to talk more about things, people, ideas, and everything I love (If I do only one thing in the next twenty-one days, this alone will change my life!)
○ _____
○ _____

> *My wish isn't to mean everything to everyone*
> *but to mean something to someone!*—*Anonymous*

—Cut————————————Signs under Heaven————————————————

Day 13: A change of feeling is a change of destiny.   —Neville Goddard

36

Wish

I am five years old, and my wishes are that my dad is nicer to me, that people are more loving to each other, and that there is world peace. My teacher said I should wish for a bike or something like that, but I already have a bike, so I'm sticking with these.

— S., a very bright young star

It was a lot harder than I thought to end this with Kevin. Sometimes he follows me and hangs around the mall where I work. I decided to move home with my parents for a while. I wish I had never met him. My parents are so happy that I didn't marry him—so are my girlfriends. I'm slowly getting my life back and starting to feel more like me.—Emma; taking karate classes

Today, do three things 4good4ever (4 Wishing):

❶ for love, something from your heart; ask someone what his or her wishes/dreams are.

Write it here:_____

❷ for life, something that supports life; wish in a fountain.

Write it here:_____

❸ for light, something for light; make a wish on a star.

Write it here:_____

Review your Personal Fortune from Day 1 in your journal and share with a friend! Your heart is not living until it has experienced pain ... the pain of love breaks open the heart, even if it is as hard as a rock.—Hazrat Inayat Khan

DAY 14

First, Value Yourself!

Men may doubt what you say,
but they will believe what you do. —*Lewis Cass*

On this day, I will respect myself, value myself, and love myself without judgment; it's only twenty-one days!

With your journal friend, share a list of five things you value about each other.

In the next twenty-one days, I want to:

○ determine what I value (honesty, patience, etc.)   ○ make a list of what I value in others
○ make a list of what I value in myself and determine   ○ ask friends what they value
   if I am living congruently with my values   ○ give away something that benefits another
○ _____   ○ _____

Today, do three things that value you.

Live in truth, be determined, live your goals, and be creative.

—Cut————————Signs under Heaven————————————

Day 14: No one can make you feel inferior without your consent.   —Eleanor Roosevelt

Value Yourself

What you think means more than anything else in your life. More than what you earn, more than where you live, more than your social position, and more than what anyone else may think about you.—George Adams

What do you value? Honesty, compassion, determination, etc.? Your heart and what you send out? Fill it in to make it yours. Example: I value hope, love, discipline, and laughter.

_____

_____

_____

_____

_____

_____

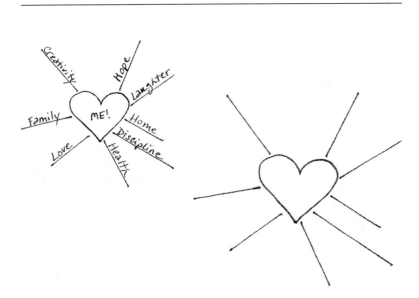

Love is the most powerful and still most unknown energy in the world.

—Pierre Teilhard de Chardin

Each day, there will be ideas, so do what you want.

Today, do three things 4good4ever:

 for love, something from your heart

❷ for life, something that supports life

❸ for light, something for light

My Rite of Passage

Week Three

Day 15: Direction ... feather

Day 16: Listen

Day 17: Glue ... stamp

Day 18: Strength

Day 19: Hope ... seed

Day 20: Celebrate ... flowers

Day 21: Love yourself

DAY 15

MY RITE OF PASSAGE

First, move in a direction for good.
Stay the path you're on and stay committed, focused, and strong.
Follow your heart.
List your options, and test with your thinking/head and with your feelings/heart.

DO: Find and carry a feather, which represents your path.

With your journal friend, talk about personal direction. Where are you going?

In the next twenty-one days, I want to:

Act as if what you do makes a difference. It does.
—*William James*

—Cut————————Signs under Heaven————————————
Day 15: The past is a prison for those who live in it.   —Anonymous

42

Direction

> Small steps ... They don't have to be big steps;
>
> they just have to head in the right direction. —Tom Clancy

My life is so undecided. I wish I knew what to do. I graduate from college in one month, and I have no job prospects. I will just breathe!

—Karin, age twenty-two; loves yoga and wide-open spaces

After three years of dating, my boyfriend, Peter, insisted marriage would ruin our great relationship. It started to be a fight that was separating us. We are both very strong-willed people, yet it is also our convictions that make us who we are, so it is important that we stay true to ourselves. In my heart, I knew I wanted a sacred marriage. I decided to "reverse the engines." —Julie, age twenty-seven; works in cosmetic sales

Today, do three things 4good4ever (4 Direction):

❶ for love, something from your heart; join a club, be involved in something you believe in.

Write it here:_____

❷ for life, something that supports life; start and write your story in your diary.

Write it here:_____

❸ for light, something for light; look at the clouds and make a picture of your future.

Write it here:_____

DAY 16

First, Listen!

If you want to be listened to, you should put in some time listening.
—Marge Pierey

Do you listen to yourself? What are you saying? Do you listen to others? What are they saying?

DO: Listen to everyone and everything around you. Listen to silence, music, and birds singing.

With your journal friend, share your favorite songs.

In the next twenty-one days, I want to:

- ○ ask questions of myself and listen to my answers
- ○ ask questions of my friends, read between the lines, and ask again
- ○ ask questions of my family and find out something new
- ○ ask questions of coworkers/students to discover something I didn't know
- ○ ask questions of my neighbors (What are they really saying?)
- ○ listen to everything around me, especially the music I love
- ○ _____
- ○ _____

—Cut——————————Signs under Heaven————————————
Day 16: The word "listen" contains the same letters as the word "silent."

—Alfred Brendel

Listen

Real communication happens when we feel safe.

—Ken Blanchard

My son loves to talk and talk. Sometimes I just imagine I'm listening to his heart instead of all the words and I just smile! — S. G., age thirty-two; loves popcorn and cats

Peter and I had a long talk. I listened to all his concerns, and rather than me disagreeing with him, to his surprise, I agreed with everything he said. I agreed that what he said was true for him. Then I told him what was also true. "If you really are so against marriage, then it's best that you not get married. And it's surely best for me to not marry you."

—Julie, age twenty-seven; loves roses and cooking Italian food

When we put ourselves in the other person's place, we're less likely to want to put him in his place. — Farmer's Digest

Today, do three things 4good4ever (2 Listen):

❶ **for love,** something from your heart; ask questions and listen.

Write it here:_____

❷ **for life,** something that supports life; be patient and wait for answers.

Write it here:_____

❸ **for light,** something for light; look for good in what people say.

Write it here:_____

DAY 17

First, Glue

What needs glue in my life?

- [ ] My health/relaxing/exercising?
  - [ ] My family/friends?
    - [ ] My career? Creativity?
- [ ] My giving back/service?
  - [ ] My education/learning new things?
    - [ ] My spiritual growth?

Follow your heart. Mend a quarrel.

Search out a forgotten friend.

Replace a suspicion with trust.

DO: *Stick a postage stamp on a reminder of what you want to glue.*

With your journal friend, share what you want to stick to.

In the next twenty-one days, I want to:

What do we live for; if it is not to make life less difficult for each other.—George Eliot

—Cut————————Signs under Heaven————————————————

Day 17: Be like a postage stamp. Stick to something until you get there.   —John Billings

Glue

> One can never speak enough of the virtues, the dangers,
>
> the power of shared laughter.—Francoise Sagan

I work with five women, and every Monday morning, we all share something about our weekends. We make sure everyone is included. It's such a little thing, but I look forward to it. It's a little "glue" that keeps us caring about each other.

—Morgan, age twenty-nine; dental hygienist, loves white smiles

After our "big" talk, Peter and I both started laughing. After months of fighting, we now agreed with each other. We agreed to spend his birthday together since our plans had been made for the next week. We had so much fun together walking in the fall leaves and enjoying all the things we had in common. We were no longer against each other; we were on the same page. Our beliefs are different, and we agree that they are.

—Julie; has a cat named Milo and a dog named Otis

Today, do three things 4good4ever (4 Glue):

❶ **for love,** something from your heart; give a loved one an extra-squeeze hug.

   Write it here:_____

❷ **for life,** something that supports life; whisper kind words to a friend.

   Write it here:_____

❸ **for light,** something for light; call someone and ask how he or she is with no other agenda.

   Write it here:_____

DAY 18

MY RITE OF PASSAGE

Strength

Character cannot be developed in ease and quiet.

Only through experience of trial and suffering

can the soul be strengthened, ambition inspired,

and success achieved.—Helen Keller

Ways I feel strong:
- ○ having a voice
- ○ being determined
- ○ acting on my dreams
- ○ meditating
- ○ respecting others
- ○ _____

- ○ keeping my promises
- ○ exercising my body
- ○ respecting myself
- ○ making healthy choices
- ○ working on a goal
- ○ _____

Do: Define and develop the strength of your character.

Character includes honesty, fairness, ethics, and integrity.
Wisdom includes good judgment and discernment.
Flexibility includes adapting to changing circumstances and letting go of courses of action that aren't working.

Character is power.—Booker T. Washington

—Cut————————Signs under Heaven————————————

Day 18: Some people think it's holding on that makes one strong. Sometimes it's letting go.
—Sylvia Robinson

Strength

Perseverance is the hard work you do after you get tired
of doing the hard work you already did.

—Newt Gingrich

People just do not appreciate trees enough in this world. They give us shade, fruit, strength, and roots. I love trees! I have fifteen grandchildren, and I have taught them all to value the "tremendous tribute of trees."
— Lorna, age eighty three; writer, grandmother, and great-grandmother extraordinaire

In the last few months, I joined a biking club and attended some social events in my church, neighborhood, and community. I met new people, yet I missed Peter, and it was easy to compare others to Peter. He sent me a text, yet I didn't answer. I knew I had to hold strong. If I wanted a new life, I had to make the changes.

—Julie, age twenty-seven; taking cooking and Italian classes

Today, do three things 4good4ever (4 Strength):

❶ for love, something from your heart; finish a project you've been putting off.

Write it here:_____

❷ for life, something that supports life; write an exercise plan and stick with it.

Write it here:_____

❸ for light, something for light; meditate alone or with a friend.

Write it here:_____

Character consists of what you do on the third and fourth tries.

—James Michener

DAY 19

First, Hope!

Determine that the thing can and shall be done
and then we shall find the way.—Abraham Lincoln

Hope can survive being the tiniest seed with little dew and tired soil and yet it blooms.

DO: Make a Hope Chest and fill it with things you want to do: cookbooks to learn cooking, maps of places you want to travel to, and hobbies you want to start. Collect anything that makes you hopeful and happy.

With your journal friend, share something for each other's hope chests.

In the next twenty-one days, I want to:

○ give hope to someone I have not previously done so
○ give hope to a situation I have not previously done so
○ give hope to a new person/situation in my life

Even a small star shines in the darkness.—*Finnish proverb*

—Cut————————Signs under Heaven————————————

Day 19: We are not held back by the love we didn't receive in the past but by the love we're not
extending in the present.
—Marianne Williamson

50

Hope

The greatest good you can do for another is not just to share your riches but to reveal to him his own.—Benjamin Disraeli

When my daughter was born, she was premature and very sick. I was afraid to be hopeful because I didn't think I could survive if she died. My husband told me to tell the fear to "go away" because this was our time for "hope." We just celebrated our baby Jasmine's tenth birthday. —Bonnie, age thirty-four; sings in the church choir

After Christmas and New Year's, Peter called and asked if we could get together for coffee. It had been my birthday and he gave me a beautiful card. Inside he wrote, "You are the only woman I have ever respected and valued." We talked about some of our long-term beliefs; many are the same. We are just in different time zones. Even if he is not meant to be my husband, he is such a great guy.

—Julie, age twenty-eight; planning a trip to Italy with girlfriends

Today, do three things 4good4ever (4 Hope):

❶ for love, something from your heart; write a hope note and put it in a friend's purse or book.

Write it here: _____

❷ for life, something that supports life; bake a cake with the word *hope* written on it and share it.

Write it here: _____

❸ for light, something for light; ask someone to hope with you.

Write it here: _____

Nothing is impossible to a valiant heart.—Jeanne D'Albret

DAY 20

First, Celebrate

Now and then, it's good to pause in our pursuit of happiness
and just be happy.—Guillaume Apollinaire

If one speaks or acts with a cruel mind, misery follows,
as the cart follows the horse.
If one speaks or acts with a pure mind, happiness follows,
as a shadow follows its source.—The Dhammapada

Love makes the world go 'round. Give love and see what happens.

In the next twenty-one days, I want to:

Have a celebration party (for any reason).

—Cut—————————Signs under Heaven———————————
Day 20: So many of our dreams seem impossible, then improbable, then inevitable.
—Christopher Reeve

Celebrate

Only one thing has to change for us to know happiness
in our lives: where we focus our attention.—Grey Anderson

The only way to enjoy anything in this life is to earn it first.
—Ginger Rogers

I had been home from Italy about two months when the doorbell rang.
The roses were beautiful, long-stemmed, in every color of the rainbow. The
attached card read, "I hope you still love roses; do you still love me? Please
say 'yes!' Will you please marry me? Peter." Every time I tell the story, I cry
and that was almost two years ago now. P.S.: The wedding was beautiful!
—Julie, age thirty; celebrating the holidays with hubby and pets

Today, do three things 4good4ever (2 Celebrate):

❶ for love, something from your heart; give flowers to someone and yourself.

Write it here:_____

❷ for life, something that supports life; congratulate someone on something earned.

Write it here:_____

❸ for light, something for light; make lists of the good in yourself and others and keep adding to it.

Write it here:_____

This very moment is a seed from which the flowers
of tomorrow's happiness grow.—Margaret Lindsey

DAY 21

First, Love yourself

See to do good, and you will find that happiness will run after you.

—James Freeman Clarke

DO: Respect yourself, value yourself, love yourself.

With your journal friend, make a list of all your lovable traits, and review your Personal Fortune from Day 1 in your journal.

We are shaped and fashioned by what we love.—Goethe

In the next twenty-one days, I want to:

○ Smile at everyone
○ Help to feed the hungry
○ _____

○ Share what I have
○ Be generous
○ _____

Today, do three things that give love to yourself.

—Cut————————————Signs under Heaven————————————

Day 21: There can be no happiness if the things we believe in are different than the things we do.

—Freya Madeline Stark

Love Yourself

> Nobody can go back and start a new beginning,
> but anyone can start today and make a new ending. —Maria Robinson

My heart and what I send out (fill it in to make it yours, and include all you love, including health, friendships, family, home, career, and interests):

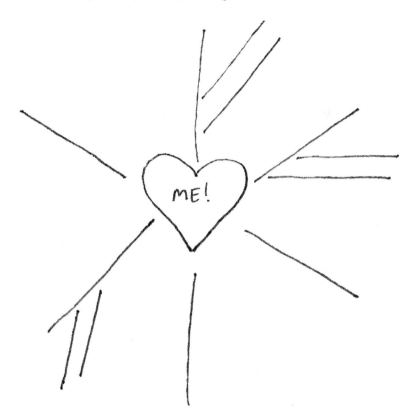

Everything (we love) matters.

To acquire love, fill yourself up with it until you become a magnet.

—Charles Haanel

Never bend your head. Look the world straight in the eye.
—*Helen Keller*

Congratulations

on your personal twenty-one-day passage.

By completing this journal, you have joined the circle of 4good4ever 'Round the World.

Name: Journal #

About the Author:

Sherry Lee Heeb is also the cocreator of Spinoza, the world's first singing and talking teddy bear; J. S. Girls Club; and a peace project for adolescents. She lives with her husband, Brian, and daughter, Natasha Joi, in a "lighthouse" on Cook's Bay in Minnesota. Sherry enjoys boating, hiking, and jogging. She can be found at Starbucks.

Sherry and Natasha Joi

For all comments and requests for additional journal copies,
please call (612) 718-7550 or
e-mail 4good4everjournals@gmail.com.
Website: 4good4everjournals.com.

The 4good4ever Journal Series:

1. Rite of Passage: Change 4 Good!

2. Cut 'Em or Keep 'Em: Building Relationships—
   Keeping What Works and Cutting What Doesn't

3. Twenty-One Gifts for Christmas: My Most Meaningful Season—
   How We Can Live What We Believe

4. Key 4 Kismet: Find What You're Looking For

5. Best Birthday Ever! What Are the Unopened Gifts from Your Birthday?

6. Happy Mother's (Every) Day! Celebrating Rays of Sunshine about Mothers

4good4ever Initiative*

*The action of taking the first step or move;
the ability to think and act in originating new ideas!

Copyright © 2012 4good4ever Journals